Blue Cows?

Rob Waring, *Series Editor*

HEINLE
CENGAGE Lear

Australia • Brazil • Japan • Korea • Mexico • Singapore • Spain • United Kingdom • United States

Words to Know

This story is set in India.
It happens in the Indian states
of Rajasthan [rɑdʒəstɑn]
and Punjab [pʌndʒɑb].

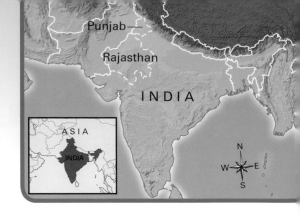

(A) **The Countryside of India.** Read the paragraph. Write the number of the correct word in **bold** next to each item in the picture. Then answer the questions.

This story is about an agricultural problem in India. It's set in the countryside of India and is about Indian **farmers** (1). The farmers **plant** (2) and grow a number of different crops such as wheat and corn. However, there are animals, called **nilgai** [nɪlgaɪ] (3), that want to eat these crops. If the *nilgai* eat the crops, the farmers lose a major source of food and income. Because of this, farmers must fight to protect their crops in the **field** (4).

5. Which of these definitions describes agriculture?
   a. the science of people interacting with animals
   b. the science of raising food
6. Which of these definitions describes crops?
   a. foods you can buy at the store
   b. foods that are grown in large amounts

The Rajasthan Countryside

B Hinduism. Read the definitions. Then complete the paragraph with the correct form of the words.

Hindu: a person who believes in Hinduism
Hinduism: an Indian religion with many gods and the belief that when something dies, its spirit returns to Earth in another body
holy: relating to a religion or a god
temple: a place where people go to show respect to a god or gods
worship: show respect for a god or gods by saying prayers or performing religious ceremonies

In India, (1)_____ is a very important religion. Because of this, people usually go to a (2)_____ every day. They go there to (3)_____ many different gods. Certain beliefs in the religion have made the cow a very important and respected animal. (4)_____ think that it is an animal of the gods. Because they think it's a (5)_____ animal, these people do not eat meat from cows, or harm them at all.

Hindus at a Temple

horse

cow

It's almost night-time in the Indian countryside. Here, in this part of Rajasthan, farm workers are very busy. No, they are not planting their fields; they are busy trying to **drive away**[1] animals. The animals are called *nilgai*, which means 'blue cow' in the language of the region.

As they walk through their fields, the farmers beat on cans and shout loudly. When they see a *nilgai*, they shout angrily and chase after it. This animal has been stealing their crops and threatening their income. They are **desperate**[2] to get the *nilgai* out of their fields.

---

[1] **drive away:** make something go away
[2] **desperate:** needing or wanting something very badly

🎧 CD 1, Track 01

In Rajasthan, there are huge groups of hundreds of *nilgai*. These animals eat everything they can find, and they especially love to eat farmers' crops.

One local farmer shows examples of the damage that the animals have done to his crops. The plants' leaves are gone; all that is left are the dead bases of the plants and dry, **trampled**[3] earth. He then goes on to explain what happens each night when the *nilgai* come. He says: "They start coming as soon as it's dark. They **stampede**[4] through the crops, eating as much as they can before we can drive them off."

---

[3]**trampled:** made flat or dug up by the feet of people or animals
[4]**stampede:** run fast

In Rajasthan, like in many places in the world, agriculture is an important part of the economy. That means that there is a growing **battle**[5] for land between people and animals. Here, it seems that the animals may be winning this battle. They're eating nearly all of the crops that humans need for food.

One farmer reports that many of the local people are giving up. They're leaving the land because of the *nilgai*. He says: "The situation is extremely bad, especially for the smaller farmers. Because the *nilgai* have come and destroyed their crops so many times, **it's not worth**[6] them planting anymore and some of them are giving up the land."

---

[5]**battle:** a fight between two forces or groups
[6]**it's not worth (doing something):** there's no need to do something because it is a waste of time or effort

Fact Check

1. How do the farmers feel about the *nilgai*?

2. Why do they feel that way?

3. What are many small farmers doing because of the *nilgai*?

9

Many farmers in Rajasthan are having a difficult time, but it is especially difficult for the smaller farmers. Many of these farmers and their families are quite poor. They totally depend on the crops that they grow. If their crops are damaged or destroyed, they may not have enough money or food to eat. So, when their crops are in the fields, these farmers watch them very carefully to protect them from being eaten. Some farmers even put their beds in the fields and sleep there. Why would they do something that is so uncomfortable? It's the best way that they can be ready when the *nilgai* come.

Rajasthani farmers often spend sleepless nights chasing the *nilgai*. It starts when the farmers see the eyes of the animals in the dark, so they know that the *nilgai* are there. Then, the animals begin running away and the chase begins. The farmers run after the *nilgai* across the fields and through **fences**[7] all night. It's a tiring solution that lasts only a short time. The farmers actually need to reduce the number of *nilgai* around their farms. It should be an easy job, but there's an unusual problem. The problem is with the animal's name.

---

[7]**fence:** structure which divides two areas; usually made of wood or metal

In the language of the region, the word '*gai*' means 'cow' and the word '*nil*' means 'blue'. Therefore the name *nilgai* means 'blue cow.' In Hinduism, the cow is an important animal that has a high place in the Hindu religion. In fact, Hindus believe that cows are holy. Since the majority of the people in India are Hindu, the cow has become a significant symbol within the Indian culture. Cows are allowed to walk freely in every city and village and people often worship cows in temples. Because of this, any animal with the word 'cow' in its name is also highly respected and considered holy— including the *nilgai*.

Since the *nilgai* is considered holy due to its name, the farmers of Rajasthan would get in trouble for harming the animals in any way. They must **put up with**[8] the animal's behavior and the loss of their crops. The interesting fact is, despite its name, the *nilgai* or 'blue cow' is not really a cow at all. It's actually a kind of **antelope**.[9] So can the name of the animal possibly provide an answer to the farmers' problems? Maybe. Although it's an unusual problem, this is not the first time that the name of the *nilgai* has caused difficulties. There's also the case of the 'blue horse'.

---

[8]**put up with (something):** continue to accept or live with something even though it's not pleasant
[9]**antelope:** a deer-like animal with long legs that can run very fast

Is the nilgai a cow?

Is the nilgai *a horse?*

Is the nilgai *an antelope?*

Predict

Answer the questions using information you know from reading to this point. Then, check your answers on pages 16 to 19.

1. Will the farmers be able to fix the *nilgai* problem?

2. If so, how will they do it? If not, why won't they be able to do it?

Fifty years ago in the Indian state of Punjab, farmers had the same problem with the *nilgai*. They gathered in a Hindu temple to look for a solution. With the help of holy men, they found the answer, and it was an extremely clever one!

The farmers of Punjab simply changed the name of the animal from *nilgai*, or 'blue cow,' to **nilgodha**,[10] or 'blue horse.' By switching the name of the problematic animals, they became 'horses'—not 'cows.' This fixed the problem because horses are not holy animals. As a result, the farmers of Punjab were able to control the number of 'blue horses,' and keep them away from their valuable crops.

---

[10]**nilgodha:** [nɪlgoʊdə]

Now, some farmers in Rajasthan want to give the *nilgai* a new name, just as they did in Punjab all those years ago. After all, if the Punjabis did it, why not them?

Is the *nilgai* a horse, a cow, or an antelope? The farmers don't know, but they do know one thing. There are more and more *nilgai* in this part of India and this is creating a lot of problems for them. For now, the 'blue cows' and the farmers must continue to fight for the crops of Rajasthan. At the moment, nobody knows just who will win the battle.

After You Read

1. On page 4, the phrase 'almost night–time' is closest in meaning to:
    A. early morning
    B. late evening
    C. midnight
    D. just before sunrise

2. In Rajasthan, the *nilgai* are everything EXCEPT:
    A. animals that eat crops
    B. animals called blue horses
    C. animals that come in big groups
    D. animals that farmers don't like

3. In paragraph 1 on page 7, 'they' means:
    A. farmers in Rajasthan
    B. farm horses
    C. a family of cows
    D. big groups of *nilgai*

4. For which group is the blue cow problem the worst?
    A. all of people in Rajasthan
    B. the *nilgai*
    C. small farmers
    D. other animals

5. People in Rajasthan may not have _____ food and money.
    A. all
    B. some
    C. enough
    D. no

6. How do the farmers feel about the *nilgai* problem?
    A. good
    B. angry
    C. terrified
    D. dangerous

7. Hindus do each of these for cows EXCEPT:
   A. worship them
   B. let them go freely
   C. think they are important
   D. hurt them

8. A *nilgai* is actually _____ type of antelope.
   A. a
   B. the
   C. any
   D. an

9. In paragraph 1 on page 16, the word 'state' means:
   A. countryside
   B. region
   C. city
   D. village

10. What did the people of Punjab do in a Hindu temple?
   A. They looked for a holy man.
   B. They created the *nilgai* problem.
   C. They fixed the *nilgai* problem.
   D. They changed the *nilgai* name to 'blue antelope'.

11. What do the farmers in Rajasthan think a *nilgai* is?
   A. a horse
   B. a cow
   C. an antelope
   D. They don't know.

12. The writer probably thinks that the *nilgai* problem in India will:
   A. grow
   B. get smaller
   C. disappear
   D. improve

EXPLORING OUR WORLD

an Interview with Professor Charles Baker

Judy: Hello, everyone! This is Judy Jamison here with our weekly science program, Exploring Our World. This week we're happy to welcome Professor Charles Baker. He's going to tell us about the holy cows of India. So to start us off, can you give us a little background about why cows get such special treatment in India?

Professor Baker: Certainly, Judy. Hinduism has been an important religion in India for many centuries. Many Hindus believe that all animals are holy, but the cow is considered especially holy.

Judy: Do you have any idea why that is?

Professor Baker: There are probably two main reasons. One is that there is an important story in the ancient Hindu texts about a cow who answers people's prayers. Also, some ancient Hindu gods were thought to show themselves in the form of cows. And one very important god, Krishna, was said to appear to people as a cowherd, which is a person who cares for cows.

Judy: Here in the West we certainly don't worship cows.

Professor Baker: I know, but there is a completely different attitude in India. Throughout history, almost every Indian family has owned a cow. They have often given them names and treated them like pets. Since cows also give the family milk, one of the most important foods, they have received double the respect.

Today there are about 14 million people and 40,000 cows walking around Delhi.

Judy: I've also heard that cows don't stay in the fields. They can go anywhere they want to. Is that true?

Professor Baker: Yes, it is. It's part of the special treatment, but as cities have become more crowded, it has created real problems. Today there are about 14 million people and 40,000 cows walking around Delhi. Can you imagine what that's like?

Judy: No, I can't!

Professor Baker: There are 100 men in Delhi whose only job is to very gently catch problem cows and take them to a safe place outside the city.

Judy: That's an interesting concept. Let's talk more about that after our break …

CD 1, Track 02

Word Count: 333
Time: _____

Vocabulary List

agriculture (2, 8)
antelope (14, 15, 19)
battle (8, 19)
crop (2, 4, 7, 8, 11, 14, 16, 19)
desperate (4)
drive away (4)
farmer (2, 4, 7, 8, 9, 11, 12, 14, 15, 16, 19)
fence (12)
field (2, 4, 11, 12)
Hinduism (3, 14)
Hindu (3, 14, 16)
holy (3, 14, 16)
it's not worth (doing something) (8)
nilgai (2, 4, 7, 8, 9, 11, 12, 14, 15, 16, 19)
plant (2, 4, 7, 8)
put up with (something) (14)
stampede (7)
temple (3, 14, 16)
trampled (7)
worship (3, 14)